MW00916655

COLLECTAFACT™

WORDS AND PICTURES THAT WORK TOGETHER

DESERTS

TWO-CAN™

PRINCETON ■ LONDON

What's in this book

*All words in the text which appear in **bold** can be found in the glossary*

What are deserts?

Deserts are dry, **barren** places where there is very little rain. Scientists call a region a desert if it receives less than 10 inches (25cm) of rain or snow each year. They also examine the type of soil and vegetation in an area.

Many of the world's deserts are in hot areas, where the temperature often soars to above 86°F (30°C). But some deserts, such as the Gobi Desert in Asia, are extremely cold. In winter, the temperature in the coldest deserts can drop to 10°F (-12°C).

The areas around the North and South are also classified as deserts and they a certainly cold!

Sand covers about ten percent of des areas. Other desert landscapes have gr rocks and mountains, or, in the polar regions, ice.

►These sand dunes are in the Namib D of southwest Africa.

▼A map of the world's major deserts.

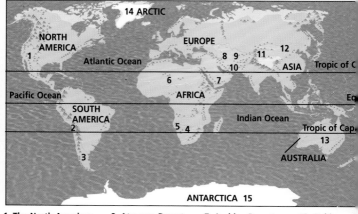

1. The North American deserts: the Great Basin, the Sonoran, Mojave and Chihuahuan Deserts, and Death Valley.
2. Atacama Desert
3. Patagonian Desert
4. Kalahari Desert
5. Namib Desert
6. Sahara
7. Arabian Desert
8. Kyzyl Kum
9. Karakum
10. Thar Desert
11. Taklimakan Desert
12. Gobi
13. Australian Desert
14. Arctic
15. Antarctica

How do deserts form?

Many of the world's deserts lie on either side of the **Equator**, in an area known as the tropics. Deserts in this area, such as the Sahara in Africa, are called **tropical deserts**. They are formed because of the movement of the air. At the Equator, the air is very warm. It starts to rise and as it does, the air cools and releases its moisture as rain. This dry air moves away from the Equator toward the tropics.

By the time it reaches the areas where the deserts lie, it has started to move back down toward the land and warm up again. This warm, dry air helps to create the desert **environment**.

DID YOU KNOW?

● The only regular supply of moistu to the Namib Desert in Africa is the fog that rolls in from the Atlantic Ocean every day.

FastFact
In the Namib desert, the dunes often reach a height of 240m. In the Kalahari desert, the sands are red, and there are hundreds of dunes.

How a rain shadow desert is formed

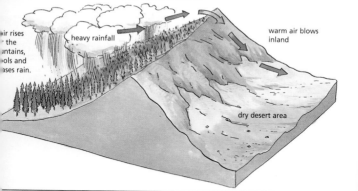

air rises over the mountains, cools and releases rain.

heavy rainfall

warm air blows inland

dry desert area

Some deserts, such as the Taklimakan Desert in China, lie in areas that are separated from the sea by mountains. Here, a **rain shadow desert** is created.

Coastal deserts, such as the Namib Desert in southwest Africa, lie near the ocean. Here, the air that moves across the ocean is cold and doesn't carry much moisture to the land. Other deserts, such as the Gibson Desert in Australia, are far inland where the air is dry.

◄ When it rains in the desert, the water may collect in channels or dry lake beds. Heavy, sudden downpours are called flash floods and they may damage the land causing erosion.

Where are the world's deserts

We often think of deserts as dry, sandy, and hot. However, several different environments fall into this category. Some areas that are called deserts can have a great deal of rain at times, while others may never have had rain at all. The Arctic and Antarctica ar covered in snow and ice, but they are s desert areas! Desert temperatures also greatly and deserts that are hot in the daytime can become really cold at nigh

▲ Most of Antarctica is covered in a layer of snow and ice known as the icecap. The icecap makes up 70 percent of all the fresh water in the world. If it were to melt, many countries in the world would be flooded.

▲ The Arabian Desert covers more than 1 million mi² (2.6 million km²) and extends across Saudi Arabia, Kuwait, Qatar, the United Arab Emirates, Oman and Yemen. The temperature ranges between 50°F (12°C) in winter and 124°F (51°C) in summer.

▲ In the Arctic, the avera temperature in the colde months of the year is -30° However, in Siberia, Russia temperature can plunge t freezing -92°F (-69°C). In t summer, the temperature rise to about 60°F (16°C).

▲ The Gobi stretches across more than 500,000mi² (1.3 million km²) of Northern China and southern Mongolia. In the winter, the temperature can drop to 10°F (-12°C). In the summer, it can rise to about 70°F (21°C).

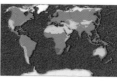

▲ The Kalahari Desert is hot, dry, and sandy. However, it can sometimes receive up to 26in (66cm) of rain in a year, so it is not always a "true" desert. The temperature ranges from 40°F (4°C) in winter to 86°F (30°C) in summer.

▲ The Karakum Desert covers an area of 135,000 (350,000km²) in central A The annual rainfall in thi region is 10in (25cm) and temperature ranges from (-4°C) in winter to 82°F (2 in summer.

◄The Antarctic is home to penguins. Penguins are black and white birds that cannot fly. Their wings are used as flippers for swimming. They move rather awkwardly on land but penguins are very graceful in water.

Atacama Desert, in Chile, driest place in the world. In ...f the Atacama, it did not ...r 400 years! On average, ...acama receives 0.5in ...) of rain per year. The ...rature ranges from 77°F ... to 86°F (30°C).

▲The Australian Desert is divided into three smaller deserts. These deserts receive between 5in (12cm) and 30in (76cm) of rain every year. The temperature may reach up to 116°F (47°C) in summer and be as low as 23°F (-5°C) in winter.

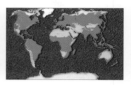
▲The Great Basin is a huge desert region in California and Nevada. It covers more than 200,000mi² (520,000km²). This area receives between 0.4in (1cm) and 2in (5cm) of rain every year. Temperatures may be between 45°F (7°C) and 135°F (57°C).

Namib Desert's name ... "place of nothing." This ... is on the coast and on ...60 days of every year ...lls in from the ocean, ...ng some moisture. ...eratures are between ...5°C) and 86°F (30°C).

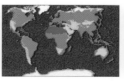
▲The Sahara is the biggest desert in the world, and it covers an area of about 3.5 million mi² (nine million km²)—about the same size as the U.S.A. The highest temperature in the world was recorded here. In 1922, it soared to 136°F (58°C).

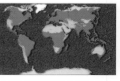
▲The Taklimakan is one of the driest deserts in the world. Less than 1.5in (4cm) of rain falls here every year. It covers about 125,000mi² (324,000 km²) in north China. The temperature ranges between 100°F (38°C) in summer and 16°F (-9°C) in winter.

Desert landscapes

The appearance of deserts varies a great deal. High mountains, shifting **sand dunes**, vast expanses of stony ground and huge boulders are all found in different deserts throughout the world. Some deserts have all these different types of landscape.

Death **Valley** in California and Nevada has dry lake beds covered in layers of glistening salt, called **salt pans**. But, in Antarctica, large areas of the land are completely covered in thick sheets of ice.

▼ Sometimes, all the sand is blown away from a desert area, leaving bare rocks.

▲ Floodwaters flowing into a desert va may sometimes become trapped and fc a lake. As the lake dries out, it leaves a layer of salt. The layers of salt build up until the whole area becomes a saltpar

▶ Some of the rock formations in the Great Basin in Nevada rise as high as 9: (300m). The landscape here has been w away over thousands of years creating columns of rock called buttes and shap the stronger rocks into flat-topped hills known as mesas.

stFact
e longest road
he world is
Pan American
hway. It runs
20mi (26,000km) from
ska to Brazil through
eral deserts.

Hot deserts

The world's largest hot desert is called the Sahara. It stretches right across the north of Africa from the Atlantic Ocean in the west to the Red Sea in the east. Altogether, the Sahara covers about 3,500,000mi² (nine million km²), which is nearly 13 times the size of Texas!

More than 10,000 years ago, the climate of the Sahara was much wetter than it is today and the region was covered with **vegetation**. But about 6,000 years ago, the climate began to change, gradually becoming much drier and turning the Sahara into a desert.

▲ Sand dunes form as grains of sand against rocks or other obstacles.

Oases

An oasis is a fertile area where underground water flows to the surface, or where there is a permanent river. There are about 90 large oases in the Sahara Desert. People live and grow crops in these areas.

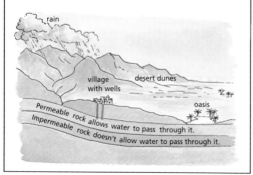

rain

village with wells

desert dunes

oasis

Permeable rock allows water to pass through it.
Impermeable rock doesn't allow water to pass through it.

Sahara is one of the hottest areas in [the] world. Temperatures of 136°F (58°C) [have] been recorded here. On average, the [Sahar]a receives less than 4in (10cm) of rain [a] year, and some areas receive as little as [1in (2].5cm).

[Th]e landscape of the Sahara Desert varies. [In th]e center, the Ahaggar Mountains rise [high]ly. In the northeast, there is a region [of roc]ky plateau known as the Tassili. Much [of th]e Sahara is sandy, however. In the [east] and west of the Sahara, there are vast [areas o]f sand called **ergs**. On the edges of [the Sa]hara there are dry **grasslands** where [few t]rees grow.

[Thi]s is an oasis. Such a fertile area [is an] unusual sight in a desert landscape.

DID YOU KNOW?

● Sand is actually tiny pieces of rock and minerals that form when larger rocks crumble away.

● Sand dunes move with the wind. Sometimes, strong winds can move a dune by up to 12in (30cm) in a day. This may mean that a settlement on the edge of a desert is gradually covered with sand, forcing the people who live there to move to another area.

● In the Sahara, some of the sand dunes are 590ft (180m) high!

● Desert travelers sometimes see a trick of light called a **mirage**. They think that they can see a pool of water in the distance. When they reach the spot, however, they find only dry sand. A mirage is created when a ray of light bends as it passes first through cold air and then through warm air.

Cold deserts

Some of the coldest places in the world are the dry deserts. The air in these areas is too cold to release any moisture, so they receive very little rain.

Antarctica is the coldest place in the world. In 1983, the temperature here dropped to -128°F (-89°C)! Most of the time, the temperature here doesn't rise above 32°F (0°C). This icy continent at the South Pole is also one of the world's driest deserts. Some parts of Antarctica don't receive any rain at all while other parts receive less than 2in (5cm) of water every year, usually in the form of snow and ice crystals.

Few plants and animals can survive in Antarctica. However, tiny plant-like creatures, known as algae, grow on the and snow. Some animals and birds, such seals and penguins, live on the coast. Th only people living in Antarctica are the 1,000 scientists who work on scientific stations there.

rctic, on the other hand, is home to groups of native people. During er, in some places around the North the temperature may reach 60°F . This is warm enough to melt the and ice. Plants burst into life and animals and birds visit to feed on the egetation. The lands of both the regions are rich in natural **minerals**. In the Arctic, people mine gold, oil, copper and tin. In Antarctica, however, mining is forbidden because it could destroy this unique **environment**.

▼ The largest penguins in the world, **Emperor penguins, can be found in Antarctica. Penguins live in colonies of many birds. Emperor penguins breed in colonies and do not build nests.**

stFact
different kinds of
nguins live in Antarctica,
only the Adélie and
peror penguins live in
s region all year round.

Desert animals

Animals that live in hot deserts have adapted to the warm, dry climate. The main problem for desert animals is the lack of water. Some animals have ways of storing water in their bodies. Others get all the moisture they need from the plants and **insects** they eat.

▼Camels can travel for days without having to eat or drink. The fat contained in a camel's hump acts like food storage and provides the animal with the energy it needs to survive.

... is a sidewinder
... with its head buried
... sand. These snakes
... sideways across the
... keeping most of their
... lear of the ground.

... gila monster is a
... f lizard found in the
... s of the U.S.A. and
... . It has sharp fangs
... venomous bite to
... y. The gila monster
... fat in its tail and
... for months
... it food.

Fact
... runners are birds that
... n the deserts of the U.S.A.
... Mexico. They are able to
... ut they prefer to run, and
... each speeds of up to 15mph (24km/h).

... ot desert animals move about at
... vhen the temperature is much cooler.
... the day, they shelter under rocks and
... or in underground burrows. Animals
... ove around in the daytime heat often
... vays of avoiding the hot sand. For
... le, kangaroo rats in the deserts of
... .A. have long back legs to hop quickly
... e ground.

... tures such as snakes and lizards, which
... d-blooded, need to warm themselves
... heat of the sun before they can move
... . They hide in the shade when the sun
... hottest.

Fennec fox
The fennec fox of the Sahara Desert has
large ears that help it to release heat
from its body and stay cool.

Desert plants

In order to survive in the harsh desert conditions, desert plants must make use of every drop of water. Plants lose a lot of water through their leaves, so in dry deserts many plants have tiny leaves that allow only a small amount of water to escape. Other plants shed their leaves during long periods when there is no rain.

Some desert plants have long, tough **roots** that reach deep underground in search of moisture. The roots of the mesquite bush in the deserts of the U.S.A. stretch 40ft (12m) below the ground! Many cacti have roots that spread over a wide area just below the surface. Water is carried up through t roots and stored in the stem of the pl

A number of plants do not grow at during periods of drought. They lie as in the soil, waiting for rain. When at rain falls, the seeds sprout quickly in damp earth and, within days, the dese covered in plants and flowers.

▼ These flowers in the Kalahari Dese have burst into life after a rare perio rain. They will bloom for only a few until the desert dries out again.

DID YOU KNOW?

● Some types of cacti can live for up to 200 years!

● The leaves of the desert holly plant grow almost vertically, or straight up. This means that the hot sunlight catches only the edges of the leaves, so they don't lose a lot of moisture.

● A type of cactus, called the jumping cholla, has stems that fall off so easily that they seem to jump on people or animals passing by!

The giant saguaro cactus is found in the deserts of the U.S.A. and Mexico. After rain has fallen, the saguaro's waxy stems swell as they fill up with water and the cactus lives on this water until the next rainfall. As much as 80 percent of a saguaro is made up of water. Some giant saguaros grow to a height of 60ft (18m).

FactFact

The witschia plants only live in the Kalahari and Namib Deserts. These two-leaved plants can live for as long as 2,000 years!

Changing shapes

Although very little rain falls in desert areas, much of the shaping of the desert landscape is caused by water. When rain does fall, it is very heavy. The hard, dry soil cannot soak up all the water, so it runs down the slopes, causing **flash floods**. The water carves out steep-sided **valleys** known as **wadis**. Rocks, boulders and pebbles are carried down from the valleys on to the desert plain.

▶This round boulder was shaped by water and the wind.

The wind also helps to shape many desert areas. Sand dunes are created by the wind. Sometimes the sand and soil are blown away completely leaving bare rock surfaces known as rock pavements. Fierce winds can blow the sand with great force and cause erosion.

Rocks on the surface of a desert are affected by the temperature, too. During the day they are heated, then at night, the rocks cool down. This constant heating and cooling weakens the rocks until, eventually, they crack.

◄ These eroded sandstone columns are in the Tassili plateaux of the Sahara.

◄ These rock formations are called badlands. They were created by the movements of wind and water. The stripes show how the sand was moved before it dried into hard layers of rock. The badlands in this picture are in the Great Basin in California.

Wadis

A wadi is created when water rushes over a dry desert slope.

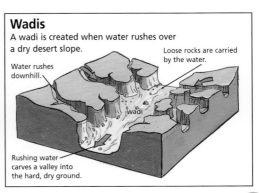

Loose rocks are carried by the water.

Water rushes downhill.

wadi

Rushing water carves a valley into the hard, dry ground.

Survival skills

Traditionally, many groups of desert people, such as the Bedouins of Arabia, were **nomads**. Instead of living in permanent homes, they moved from place to place, putting up temporary shelters wherever they stopped. Their animals provided meat and milk, as well as wool and skins which were used to make clothing and tents. The nomadic people traded with other desert groups exchanging goods such as wool, leather, rice, and grain.

Although some nomadic tribes still follow the traditional way of life, many do not. Now, most desert people spend only part of each year traveling, while others live in permanent campsites or villages near oases. One reason for this changing way of life is

that many desert people wish to move to towns and cities in search of work.

Another reason may be that some governments have made it difficult for people to travel between countries. Sev[e] **droughts** have also made it harder for nomadic people to survive.

FastFact
Most of the Patagonian Desert is much too hot and dry to grow crops. The biggest industry in the Patagonian Desert is sheep farming.

▼ This Bedouin is looking after a herd sheep and goats.

e a solar still

g a solar still is a way of collecting
from the ground. Desert travelers
uild solar stills to catch water.
weather, try making a still of
wn on a beach or in your yard.

You will need:
- a shovel
- an open-topped jar or can
- a sheet of plastic
- stones

a hole about 3ft (1m)
and 24in (60cm) deep
ace the jar or can
center of it.

ead the plastic
he hole and secure
ges with stones.

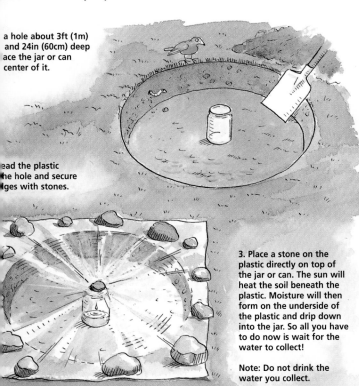

3. Place a stone on the
plastic directly on top of
the jar or can. The sun will
heat the soil beneath the
plastic. Moisture will then
form on the underside of
the plastic and drip down
into the jar. So all you have
to do now is wait for the
water to collect!

Note: Do not drink the
water you collect.

Science at work

It is very difficult to grow crops in dry desert lands. Scientists have developed several different ways of watering the ground in some deserts to make them **fertile**. People can build a network of canals to carry water from a lake or **river** to their farmlands. Or, where water lies deep underground, people can dig wells to pump water up to the surface. Watering the land in this way is called **irrigation**.

Many desert lands contain important and valuable **minerals**. Diamonds are mined in the Namib Desert in southwest Africa and there are huge copper and sodium nitrate mines in the Atacama Desert in South America. Gold, uranium, and aluminum have been discovered in the Australian Desert, while there is **oil** and natural gas in parts of the Great Basin, Sahara, and Arabian Deserts.

▲ These circular wheat in Libya are watered by pipes that move like th hands of a clock. The w is pumped from deep u the ground.

◄ Narrow ditches, calle furrows, can be dug to water between rows o crops. The water flows the furrows through pi with holes in them.

▲ This is an open-pit copper mine in the Great Basin in Nevada.

deserts receive lots of sunlight that
e collected and turned into electricity.
ethod of making electricity is called
power. One way to make solar power
ay many mirrors out over an area of
These focus the sun's rays on to a
. Then, a special fluid is heated as it
through pipes under the target. The
uid makes steam or gas that is pumped
earby power station. The heat energy
steam or gas powers turbines to
ate electricity.

Fact
only humans living in
rctica are scientists. In the
ner months, up to 1000
tists live there, studying
ocal conditions and the weather.

DID YOU KNOW?

● Each year, many of the world's
deserts grow bigger. This is partly
because of the changing climate but
the main reason is human activity.
Fertile lands around the edges of
some deserts are being made barren
by cattle or livestock grazing there
and stripping the ground of its
vegetation. Huge mining projects,
as well as cutting down trees, also
increase the size of some deserts.
This process is known as **desertification**.

The Search for the Lost City

As soon as Harry Philby heard the name Wabar, he decided that he would be the person to find this legendary lost city.

For many years, storytellers had talked of the capital of King 'Ad Ibn Kin'ad, which lay deep in the Rub' al Khali Desert in Arabia. Here, according to legend, there were palaces encrusted with gems and surrounded by beautiful gardens of exotic flowers. But one terrible day, the entire city had been destroyed by fire.

By the time Harry Philby heard the stories of Wabar, the city had been lost for more than 7,000 years. It was said to have existed on the banks of a river that had long since been covered over by the shifting desert sands. The desert in this region was known to the local people as "The Empty Quarter."

Many of them warned of the terrible dangers that lay within the desert. The sands, they said, were littered with the bleached skeletons of travelers and t

with provisions. On the first night, as Philby stood by the campfire talking, he fainted. His face turned yellow and his companions were convinced that he was going to die. They wrapped him up warmly and took turns sitting by him until morning. When he awoke, he felt perfectly well. The mystery illness had passed.

The expedition moved on. But their journey seemed to be cursed with bad luck. First, the weather turned bitterly cold so that the drinking water froze. Then, a few days later, it became unbearably hot. Grains of sand were whipped up all around the men making their faces raw. Still the camels trudged on through the sand.

It wasn't long before the water ran out. The men urgently searched for wells buried deep in the sand. At last, they were fortunate enough to find a

s who had perished there in the
ng desert heat. But Philby was
mined. He set out on January 6,
with 18 men and 32 camels loaded

well, but had to spend hours digging before they reached the water which was deep underground.

The party continued, crossing the beds of two ancient, dried up rivers. After several days, they came to a third river bed. This was, Philby believed, the river on which the legendary city of Wabar had stood.

At last, the expedition camped within only a day's journey of Wabar. Philby tossed and turned on his camp bed that night, dreaming of reaching the long-lost city. The next day the party marched on, following the river's course.

"Look!" shouted one of the men.

Philby shaded his eyes against the sun. On the crest of a distant ridge, he saw what appeared to be a low line of ruins.

Philby urged his camel on thrilled by the idea of turning his dream into reality. When he reached the top of the ridge, Philby jumped down from his

camel and ran across the sand. But t Philby sank to his knees with a groa He was looking down on the remain an old volcano! Most of the volcano

filled with sand, but its rocky edge
still be seen. Philby was almost
whelmed with disappointment.
alized that the legendary city of

Wabar still lay hidden, somewhere deep
beneath the shifting desert sands.
The next day the men demanded to
leave the area. But Philby wanted to

achieve something from the trip. Instead of heading back the way they had come, Philby ordered his weary companions to travel across 372mi (600km) of hot, waterless desert. The exhausted men pressed their thirsty camels on through the drought-stricken land. None of the men, who had lived in the desert all their lives, had ever se such a desolate place!

But finally, on March 14, over two months since the journey began, th emerged from the desert — the firs people in history to cross the Empty Quarter from side to side.

Desert fact-file

Use this page for quick reference, and when someone asks you for information.
The figures do vary from year to year, as they do anywhere, but it's interesting
to be able to compare one desert landscape with another.

Name of desert	Annual rainfall	Highest temperature	Lowest temperature
Antarctica	2in (5cm) snow	32°F (0°C)	-128°F (-89.2°C)
Arabian Desert	<4in (10cm)	124°F (51°C)	54°F (12°C)
Arctic	<10in (25cm)	60°F (16°C)	-92°F (-69°C)
Atacama Desert	0.5in (1.3cm)	86°F (30°C)	77°F (25°C)
Australian Desert	5-30in (12-76cm)	116°F (47°C)	23°F (-5°C)
Great Basin	0.5-2in (1-5cm)	134°F (57°C)	<32°F (0°C)
Gobi	<10in (25cm)	70°F (21°C)	10°F (-12°C)
Kalahari Desert	10-25in (25-66cm)	86°F (30°C)	39°F (4°C)
Karakum	10in (25cm)	84°F (29°C)	28°F (-4°C)
Kyzyl Kum	4in (10cm)	86°F (30°C)	28°F (-4°C)
Namib Desert	only fog	86°F (30°C)	59°F (15°C)
Patagonian Desert	<10in (25cm)	68°F (20°C)	43°F (6°C)
Sahara	<4in (10cm)	136°F (58°C)	54°F (12°C)
Taklimakan Desert	<1.5in (4cm)	100°F (38°C)	15.8°F (-9°C)
Thar Desert	<10in (25cm)	98°F (37°C)	60°F (16°C)

True or false?

Which of these facts are true and which are false?
If you have read the book carefully, you will know the answers!

1. **Sand** consists of tiny pieces of rocks and **minerals**.

2. All deserts are hot.

3. Most desert animals move about during the day.

4. The Sahara used to be covered with **vegetation**.

9. The temperature in a hot desert falls at night.

10. **Coastal deserts** are always separated from the sea by mountains.

11. Many desert peoples no longer follow **nomadic** way of life.

5. **Mesas** and **buttes** are types of cacti.

6. **Oases** are fertile areas in the desert.

7. Sand covers half of all desert areas.

8. A **mirage** is a trick of light.

12. Some desert plants store water in their stems.

ANSWERS: 1.T 2.F 3.F 4.T 5.F 6.T 7.F 8.T 9.T 10.F 11.T 12.T

Desert word search

Photocopy this page and see if you can solve this desert word puzzle.
All of the words listed below can be found either forwards, backwards or diagonally.
When you have found them all, you'll discover one more word!

F	E	R	T	I	L	E	W	E	B	N	P
L	S	A	L	T	P	A	N	S	U	V	L
A	L	D	R	Y	D	R	E	R	T	N	A
S	A	R	A	I	N	N	S	E	T	O	T
H	R	O	S	I	U	A	N	W	E	I	E
F	E	U	U	D	S	O	S	O	S	T	A
L	N	G	O	E	I	A	O	P	D	A	U
O	I	H	M	S	N	S	H	R	A	G	X
O	M	T	O	E	G	E	O	A	M	I	D
D	M	R	N	R	N	S	T	L	O	R	N
V	E	G	E	T	A	T	I	O	N	R	A
S	U	N	V	D	L	O	C	S	T	I	S

	dunes	flash flood	minerals	rain	sun
es	ergs	hot	nomads	saltpan	vegetation
ght	erosion	irrigation	oases	sand	venomous
	fertile	mesas	plateau	solar power	wadis

33

Glossary

bactrian camel A two-humped camel native to central Asia.

barren Land in which plants cannot grow.

Bedouin A traditionally nomadic tribe of people in Arabia.

buttes Columns of rock in desert areas that have been worn away by wind, water, and heat.

coastal desert A desert which lies near the ocean.

cold-blooded Animals whose body temperature varies according to the temperature of their environment.

desertification The process of making or becoming a desert. Desertification can happen naturally or be caused by human activities.

dromedary A one-humped camel. Also called an Arabian camel.

drought A long period of dry weather with no rainfall at all.

dune A mound or ridge of loose sand formed by the wind.

environment A word used to describe the climate and landscape, as well as human, animal, and plant life of a region.

Equator An imaginary line around the middle of the Earth, halfway between North and South Poles. Lands and seas near the Equator are warm.

ergs Huge areas of moving sand.

erosion When parts of Earth's surface are worn away by wind, water, and heat.

When referring to the land, soil that
has enough water and minerals
plants to grow.

floods Sudden, violent floods that
when heavy rain falls in a desert. If
ground is hard and dry, the water rushes
the surface instead of soaking in. The
of the water wears away the land.

land A large open area covered
grass.

An animal with an external skeleton,
antennae, three pairs of legs, and
wings. Flies, ants, and crickets are
cts.

on Methods of supplying water
areas. Building canals or digging
in order to make the land suitable
wing crops, are examples
ation.

Large, flat-topped hills, formed
ion over thousands of years.

minerals Natural, non-living substances,
such as salt or tin, that are found in
the ground.

mirage An optical illusion caused by the
heat in hot weather. In the desert, a mirage
may cause people to believe they see a
pool of water in the distance.

nomads People who have no permanent
home. Nomads travel from place to place
building temporary shelters wherever
they stop.

oasis A fertile area in a desert, where
underground water flows to the surface
or where there is a permanent river.

oil A thick liquid, found in animals, plants
and minerals. Oil is used for cooking and
as fuel.

plateau Area of high, flat land.

rain shadow desert A desert which is
shielded from rain by mountains or hills.

river A large amount of water flowing over land to the ocean or a lake and carving a channel for itself.

roots The parts of a plant that grow underground. Roots take in water and help stop the plant from falling over.

salt pan An area where water has evaporated over time leaving behind a layer of salt.

sand Tiny pieces of rock and minerals. Sand is formed when larger rocks crumble away.

sodium nitrate A type of mineral used to make matches, explosives, and fertilizers.

solar power Energy from the sun that is converted using solar panels and used to make electricity.

tropical desert A desert near the Equator which is formed by the movement of air.

valley A low area usually enclosed by and with a stream flowing through it

vegetation The tree and plant life of an area.

venomous A word to describe an ani that uses poison to kill its prey.

volcano A mountain that has an ope in the Earth's crust. Lava, rocks, and g escape from this opening. Volcanoes erupt continuously or repeatedly over

wadis Steep-sided valleys in desert ar that have been carved out by water.

well A hole in the ground from which we take water or oil. Wells can be na or manufactured.

Photocopy this sheet and use it to make your own n●

Photocopy this sheet and use it to make your own no

Draw your own desert scer

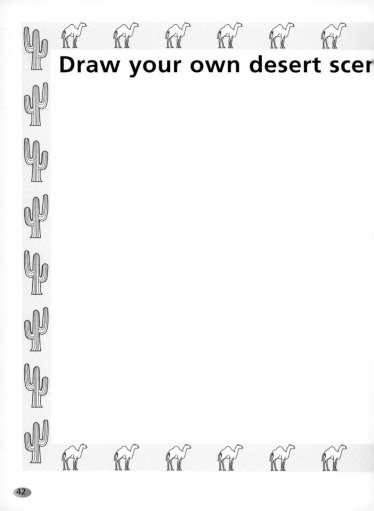

Questions and answers

Deserts are such extreme **environments** to live in, sometimes it's hard to imagine what life must be like for the animals and people that have the desert as their home. Sam the Snake and Leo the Lizard have lived in the desert all their lives, but Sam is full of questions. Luckily, Leo can give her all the answers!

Do people create deserts?

Sometimes desert areas are created by human activities. When there is too much farming, heavy mining, or if too many trees are cut down, an area may turn into a desert. This is called **desertification**.

What is desertification?

Desertification is a serious environmental problem that occurs when **fertile** lands become deserts. At the moment more than 124,000mi² (200,000km²) of new desert land

A snake can move over the hot desert sand in a special way, so that only a small area of its body touches the sand at any time.

Sam the Snake

is created every year. It's a problem bec when a fertile area becomes **barren**, m kinds of plants and animals can no long survive.

Can deserts become fertile?

Desert areas can be saved by **irrigation** systems. These transfer water from nea lakes or rivers, or from deep undergrou Trees and grasses can be planted on the edges of deserts to stop them spreadin

What is the biggest desert in the world

The Sahara is the biggest desert, coveri over 3,500,000mi² (nine million km²). C about two million people live in the Sa mostly in the more **fertile** areas around edges of the desert.

Which desert is the driest?

Antarctica is the driest desert in the wo Some scientists believe that there are p of this icy continent that have never received any rain at all!

What kinds of animals live in deserts?

Apart from snakes and lizards, there a many different kinds of desert animals. include birds, mammals, reptiles, **insect** arachnids. All the animals that live in t desert have adapted to the harsh clima one or more ways. The most well-know desert mammal is probably the camel. survive for three days, travelling about 62mi (100km) each day, without drinkin or eating.

...do camels store in their humps?
...people think that camels store water
...r humps so that they can cross the
...sert lands. But, in fact, they store fat
...r humps. This is why camels can go for
...three days without eating. As the fat
...up, a camel's humps get smaller.

...many humps does a camel have?
...daries, also called Arabian camels,
...ne hump. **Bactrian camels** have two.

...s an arachnid?
...ids are a group of animals that
...es spiders, scorpions, mites and ticks.
...scorpions are highly **venomous,** and
...quite large. You wouldn't want to
...ung by one of these desert creatures!

**...other mammals can survive in
...sert?**
...ys, foxes, rabbits, and wild cats can
...in desert conditions. Many rodents,
...mammals with strong, pointed teeth,
...very well in the desert. They mostly
...burrows, which stay cool in the heat
...day.

...o hot deserts become cold at night?
...loudy night, the sun's heat is trapped
...clouds before it can escape into the
...phere. The air in desert regions does
...ntain enough moisture for clouds
...m. This means that the sun's heat
...s, and some deserts can become
...old at night.

Reptiles, including lizards, are cold-blooded. They need to be warm in order to be active.

Leo the Lizard

What kinds of birds live in deserts?
Birds of prey, such as hawks and vultures,
do very well in the desert. They prey on the
smaller mammals that live there. Ostriches,
large birds that cannot fly, but run very well,
also live in the deserts of Africa.

What is a "desert rat?"
"The desert rats" was the nickname given
to soldiers belonging to the 7th British
armored division in the North African desert
campaign in World War II. They had
a small desert mammal, the jerboa, as a
badge. Of course, there are lots of real
rats in the desert, too!

Where does the name desert come from?
The name is from the old Latin word
"desertus," meaning something that was
left or abandoned.

Index

www.two-canpublishing.com

Published by Two-Can Publishing LLC
234 Nassau Street, Princeton, NJ 08542

Copyright © 2001, Two-Can Publishing

For information on Two-Can books and multimedia, call
1-609-921-6700, fax 1-609-921-3349, or visit our Web site.

All rights reserved. No part of this publication may be reproduced, stored in
a retrieval system or transmitted in any form or by any means electronic,
mechanical, photocopying, recording or otherwise, without prior
written permission of the publisher.

'Two-Can' is a trademark of Two-Can Publishing.
Two-Can Publishing is a division of Zenith Entertainment Ltd,
43–45 Dorset Street, London W1H 4AB.

ISBN 1-58728-757-9

1 2 3 4 5 6 7 8 9 10 03 02 01

Photograph credits: Bruce Coleman: front cover; Ardea: p.12(tr),
p.19, p.22; Bruce Coleman: p.5, pp.18–19, p.20, p.24(b), p.37; Robert Harding: p.16(b),
p.25; Hutchison: p.21; Frank Lane: pp.6–7, p.10(t); Planet Earth Pictures: p.11,
Survival Anglia: p.12(b), p.18(t), p.19; Sygma: p.26(tr), p.36(tl);
Zefa: pp.12–13, pp.14–15, p.36(br)
Illustrations on pages 8–9, 44–45 are by Michele Egar and Jon Stuart;
all other illustrations are by Francis Mosley and Linden Artists.

Every effort has been made to acknowledge correctly and contact the source of each
picture and Two-Can Publishing apologises for any unintentional errors or omissions
which will be corrected in future editions of this book.

Printed in Hong Kong by Wing King Tong

This title previously published in a large format.